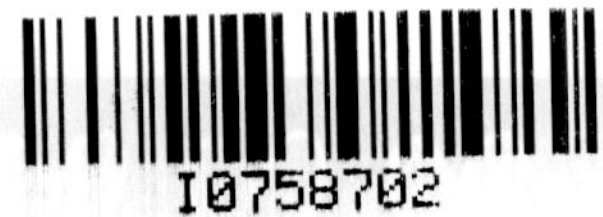

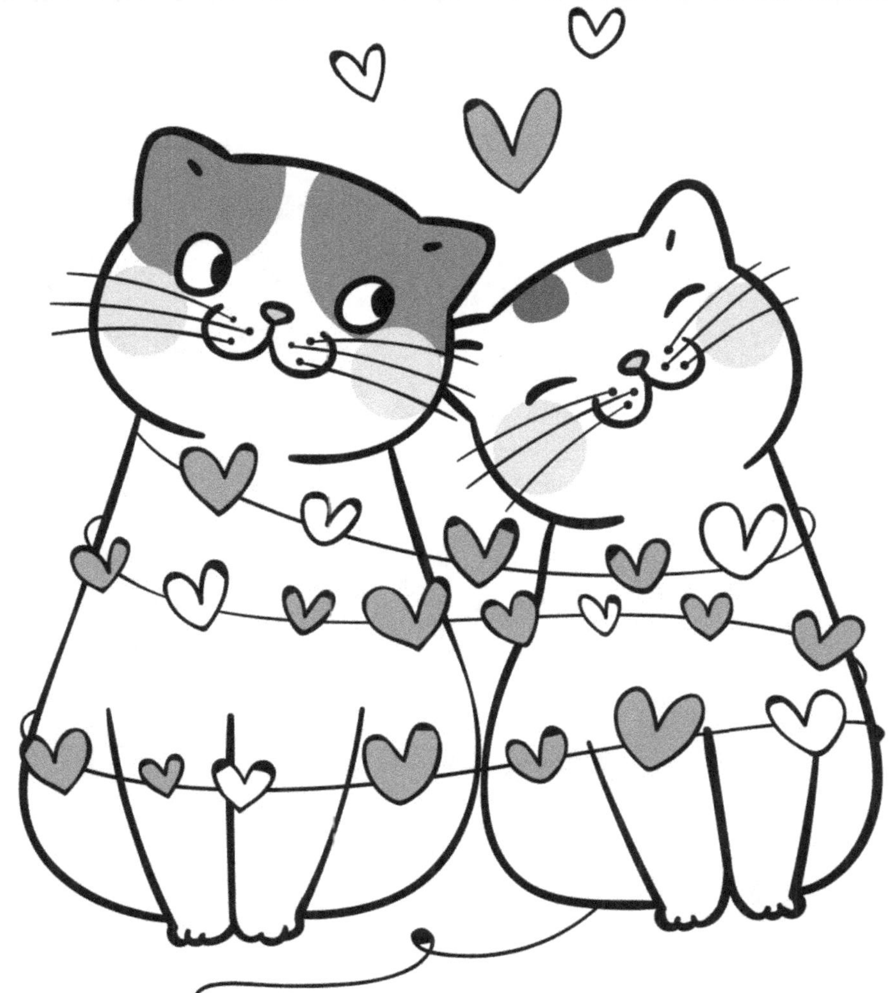

THIS BOOK BELONG TO ....

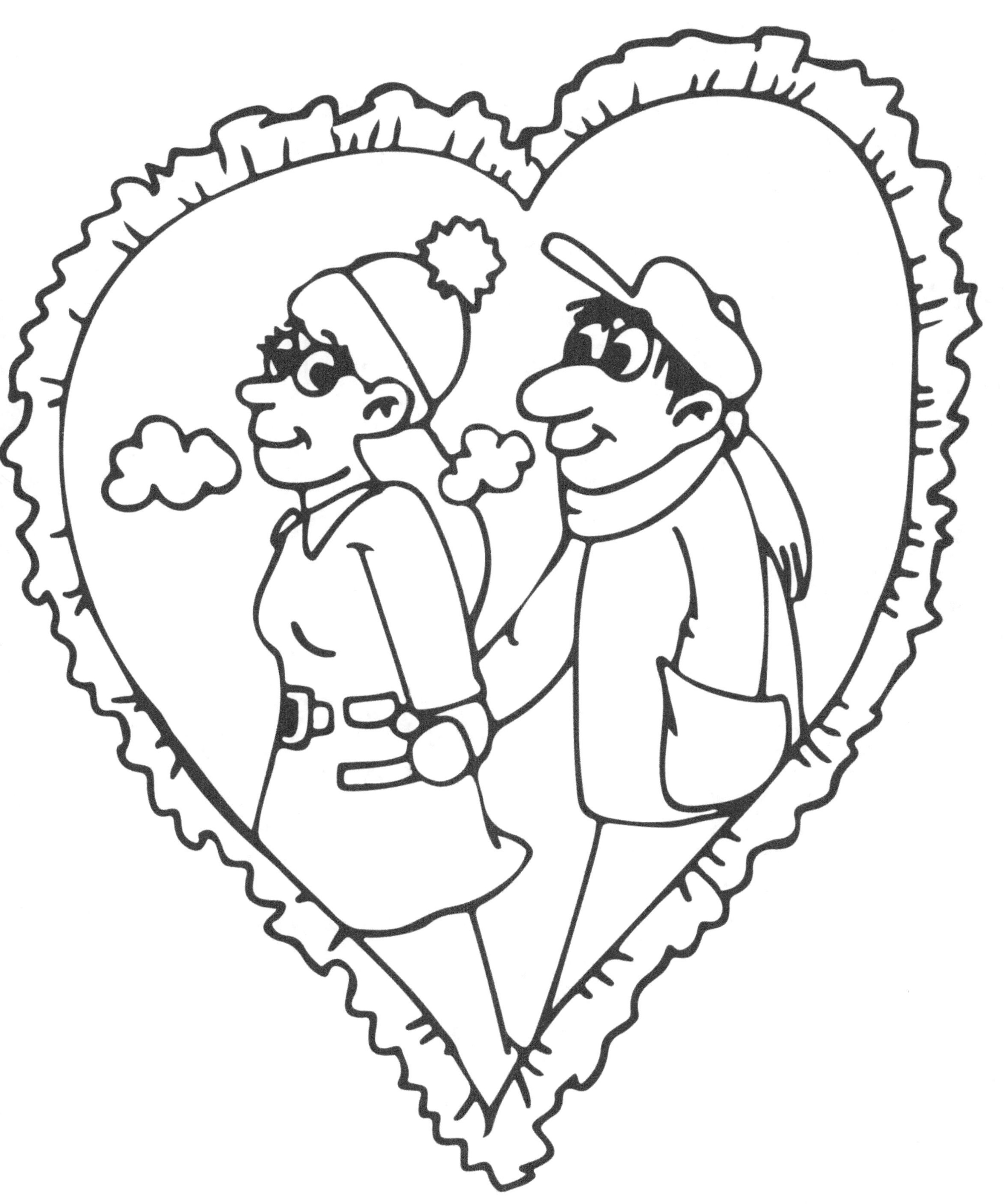

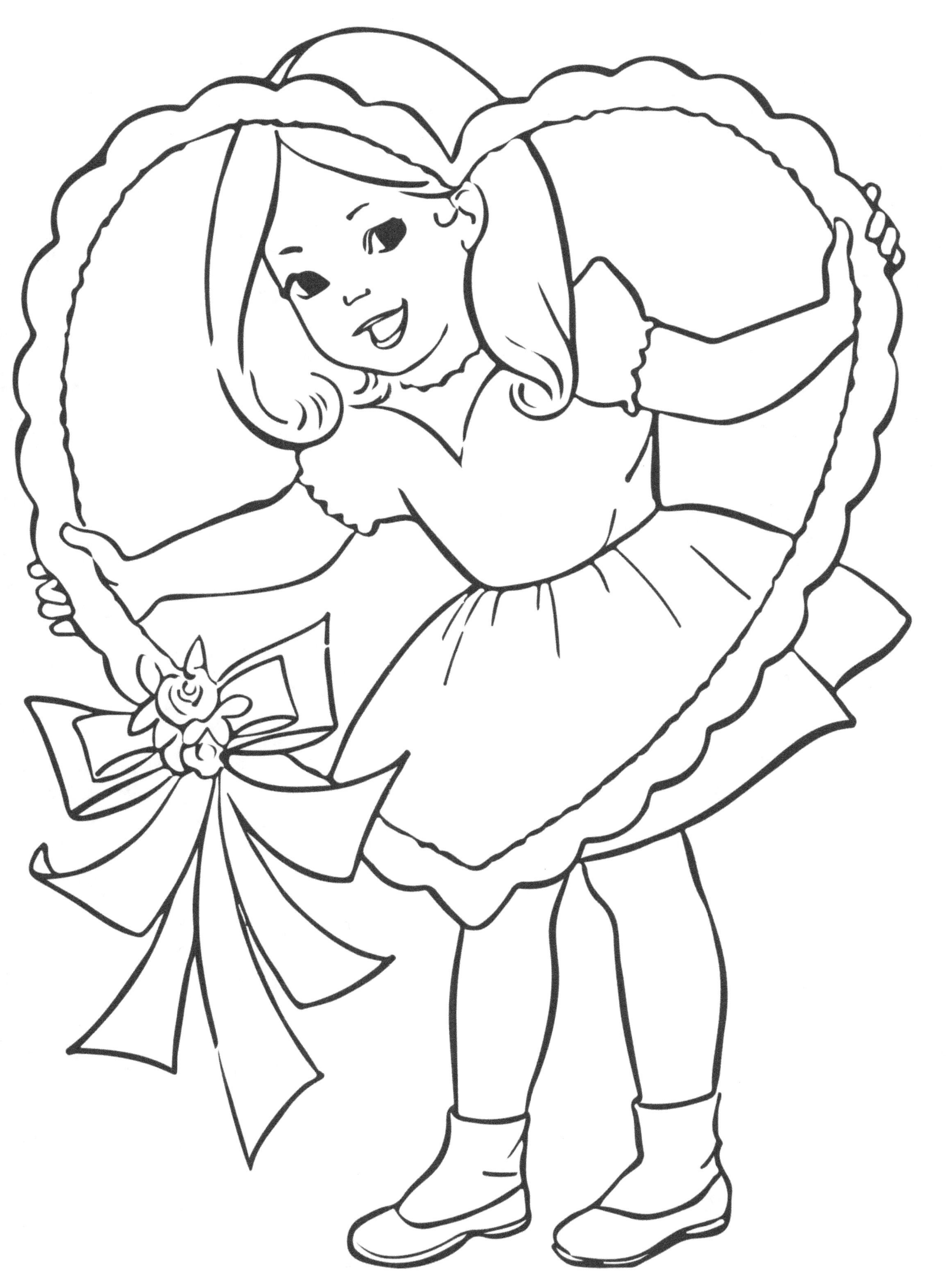

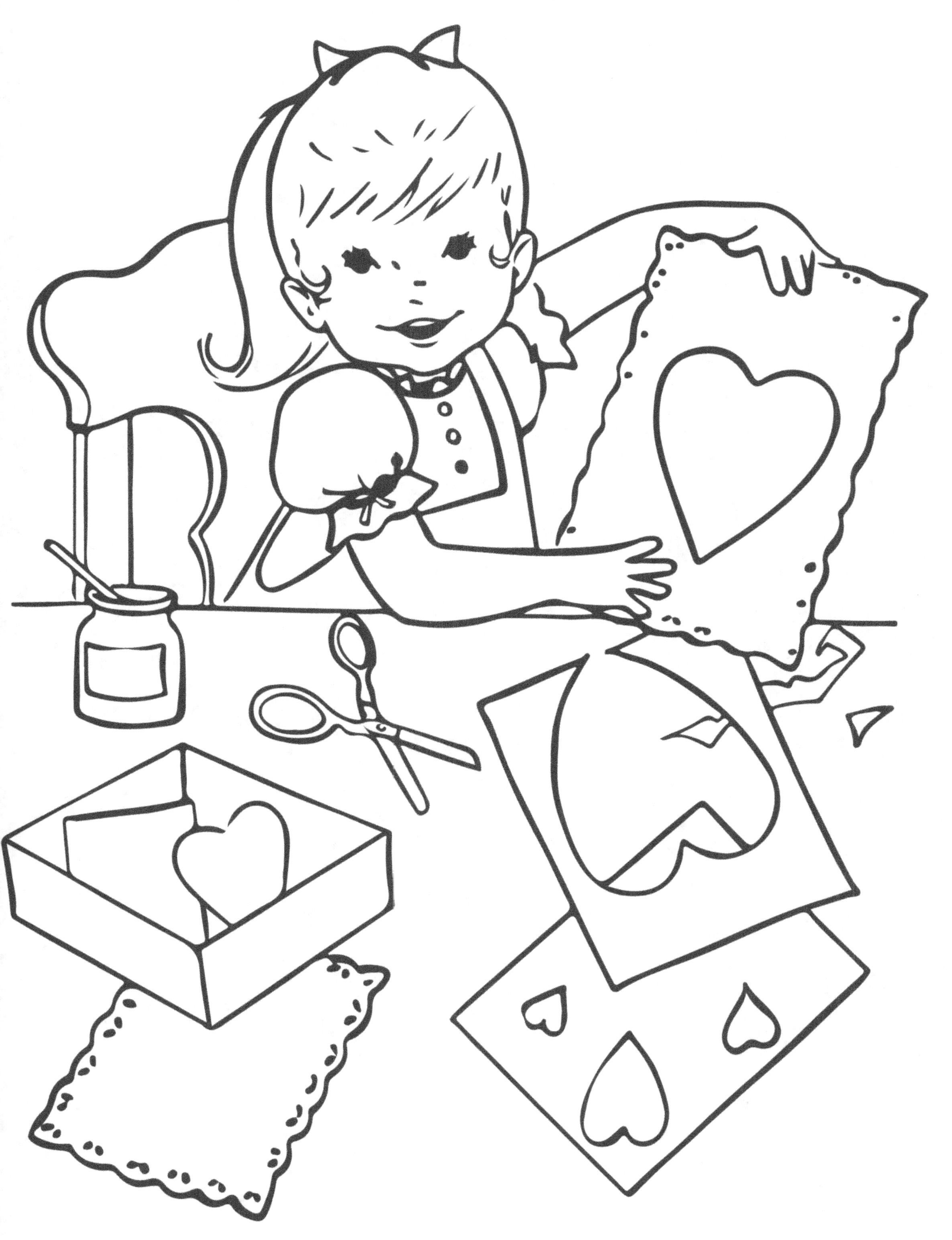

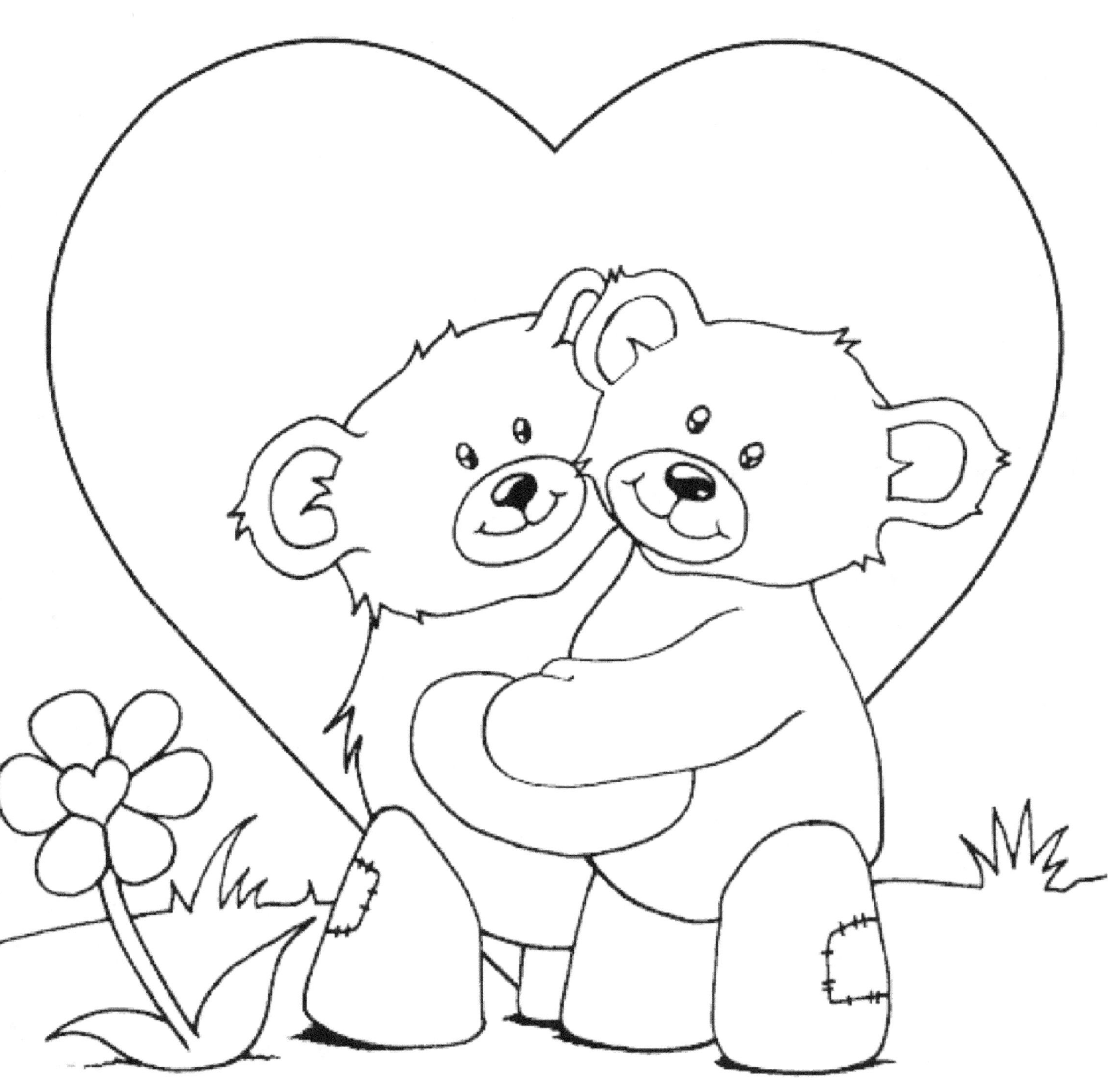

Happy Valentine's Day

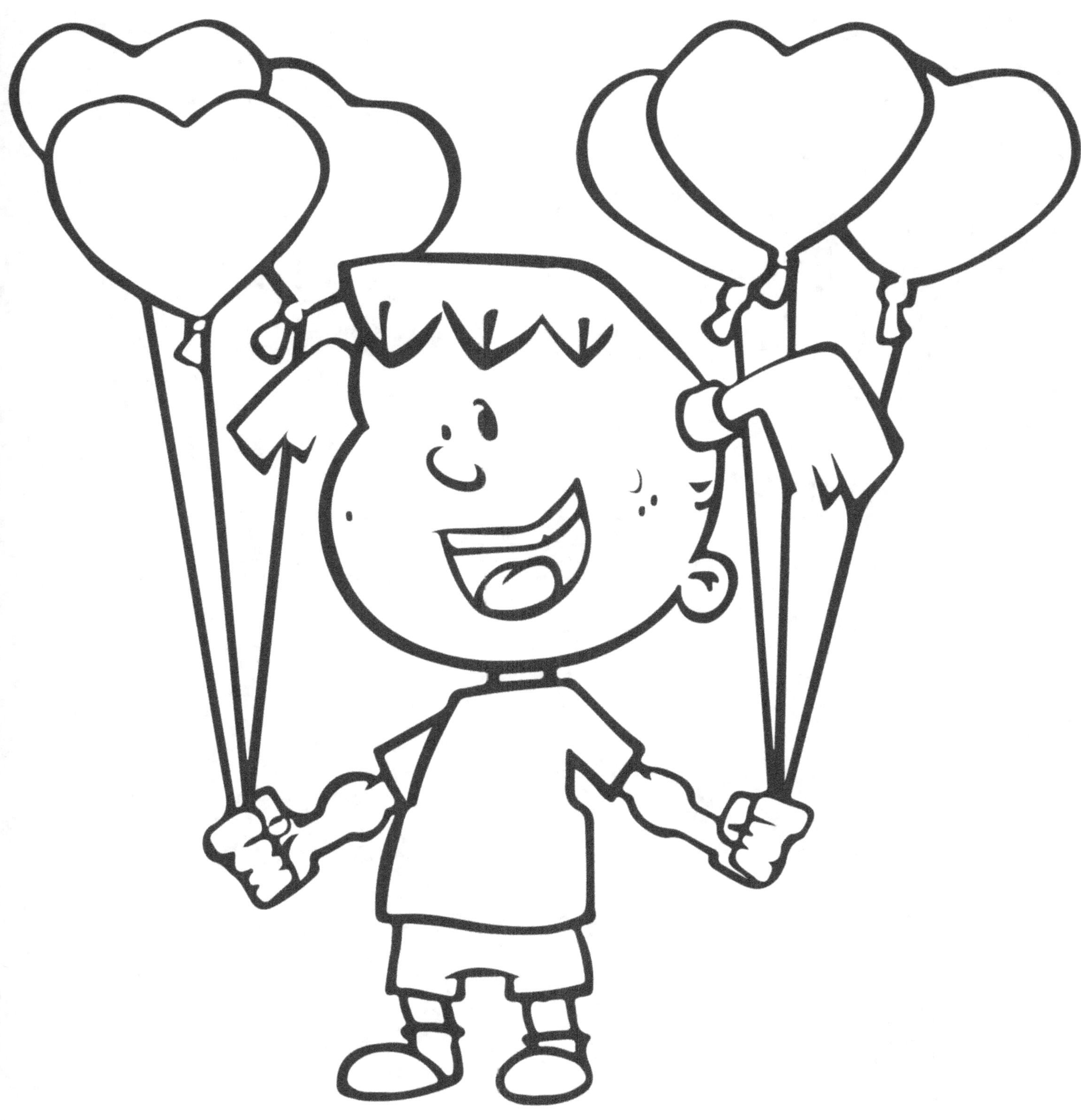

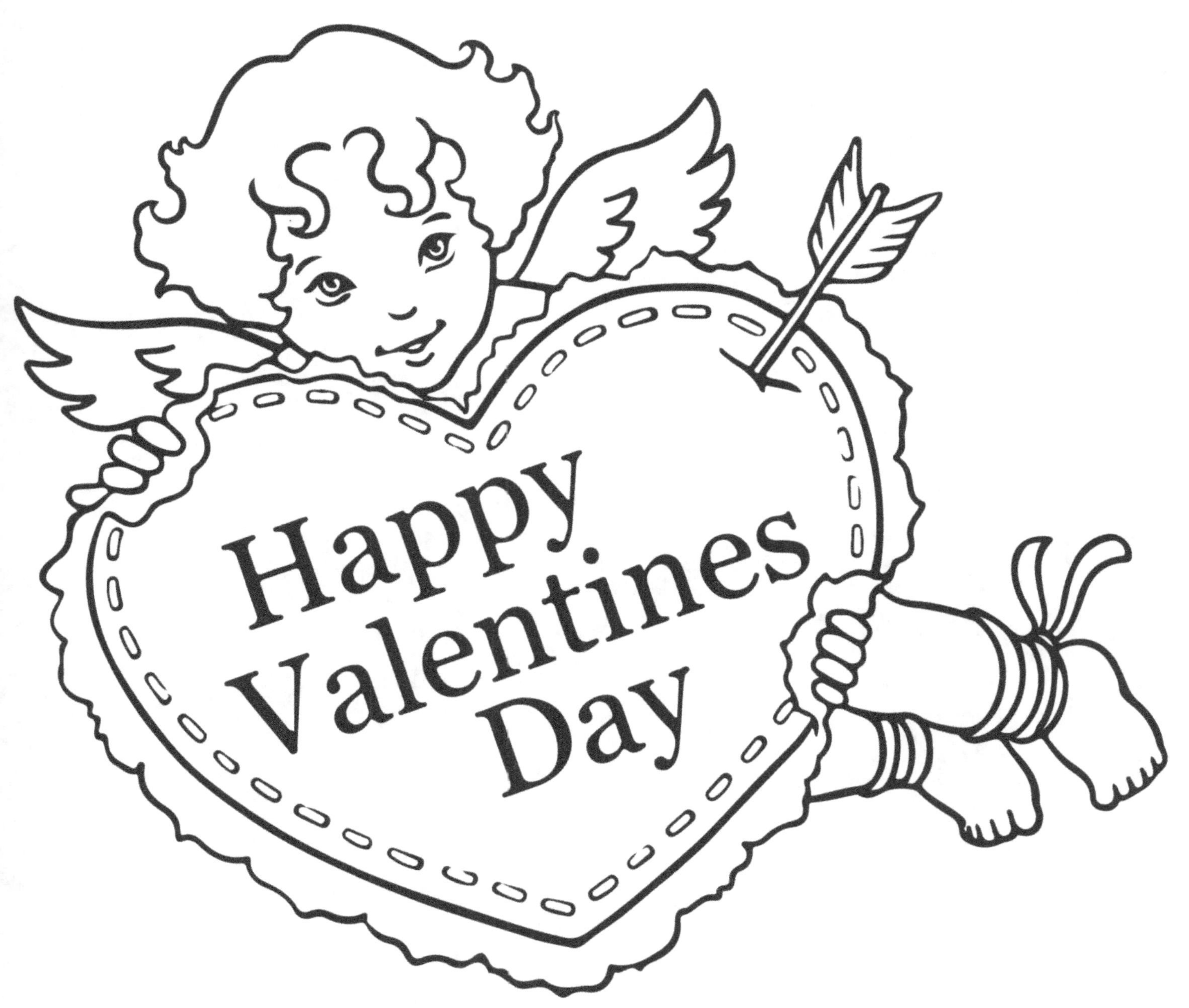

Happy
Valentines
Day

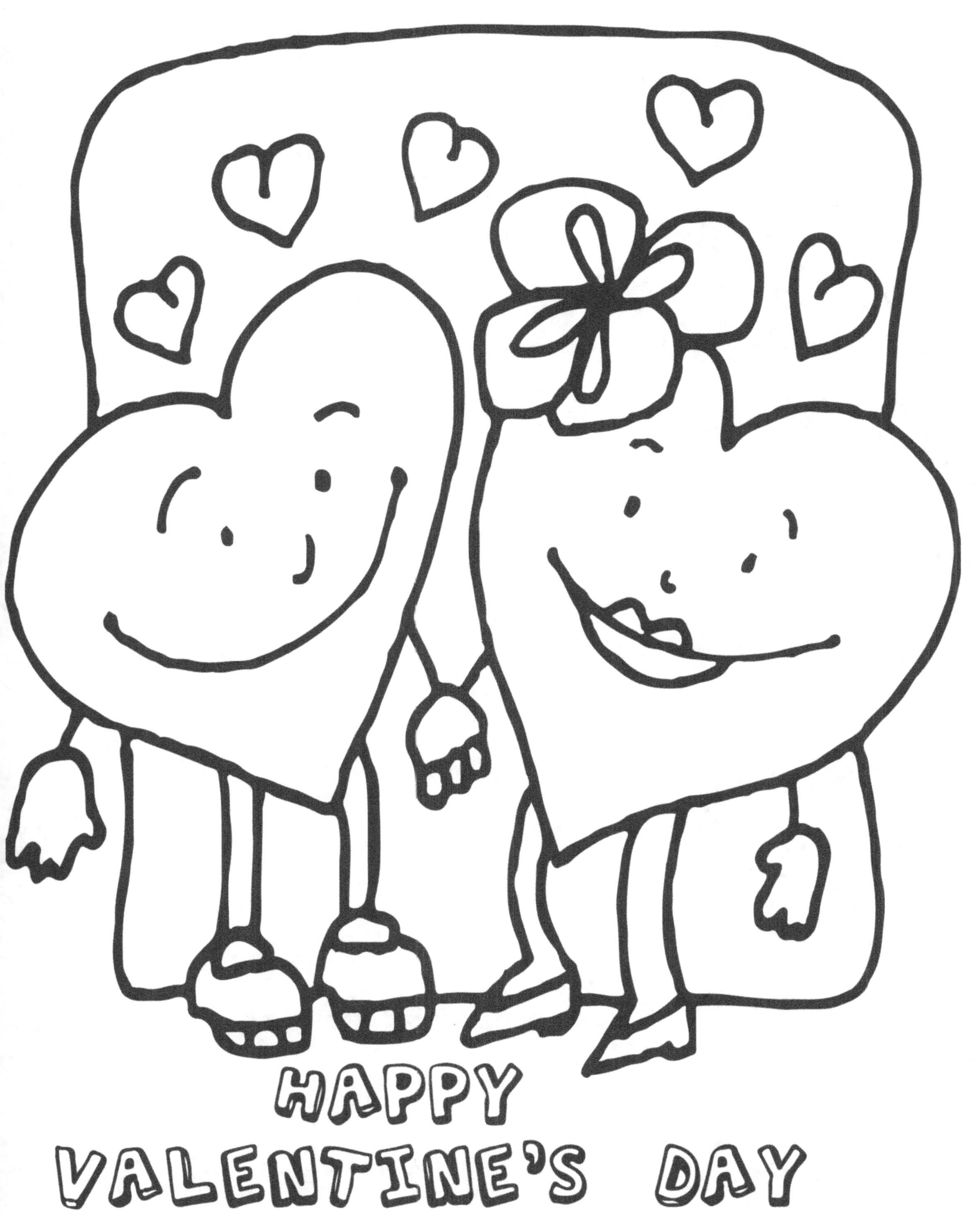

HAPPY
VALENTINE'S DAY

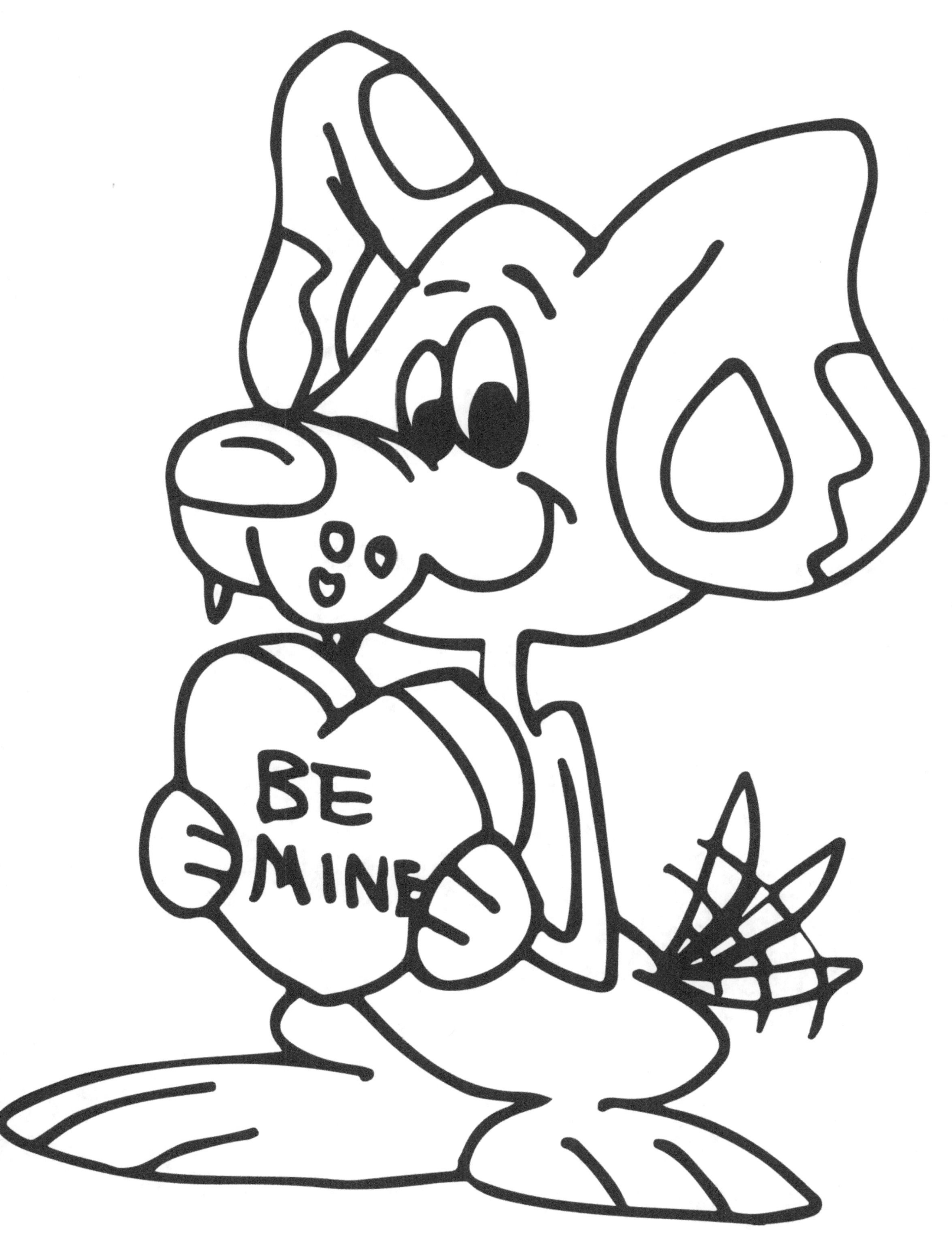

BE
MINE

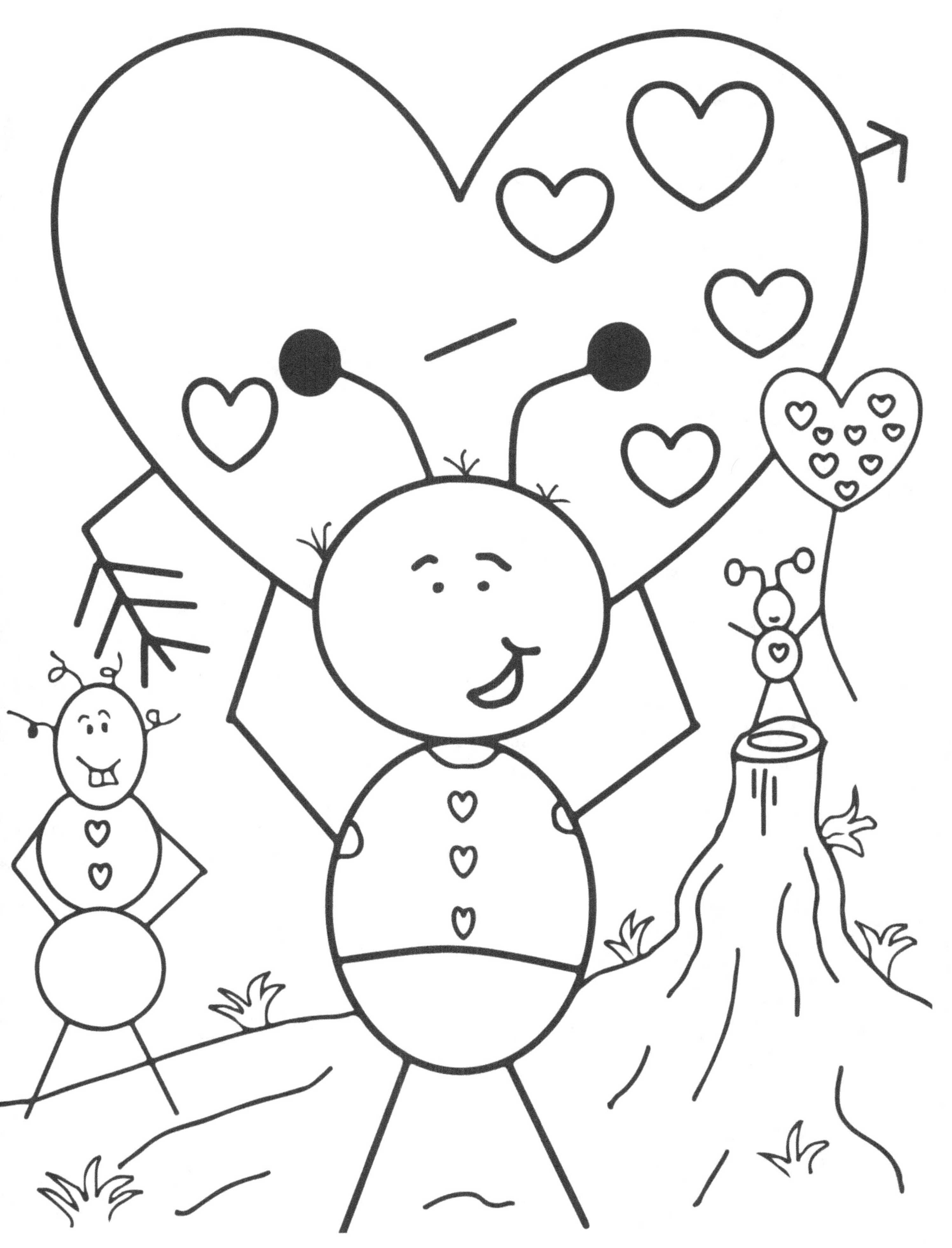

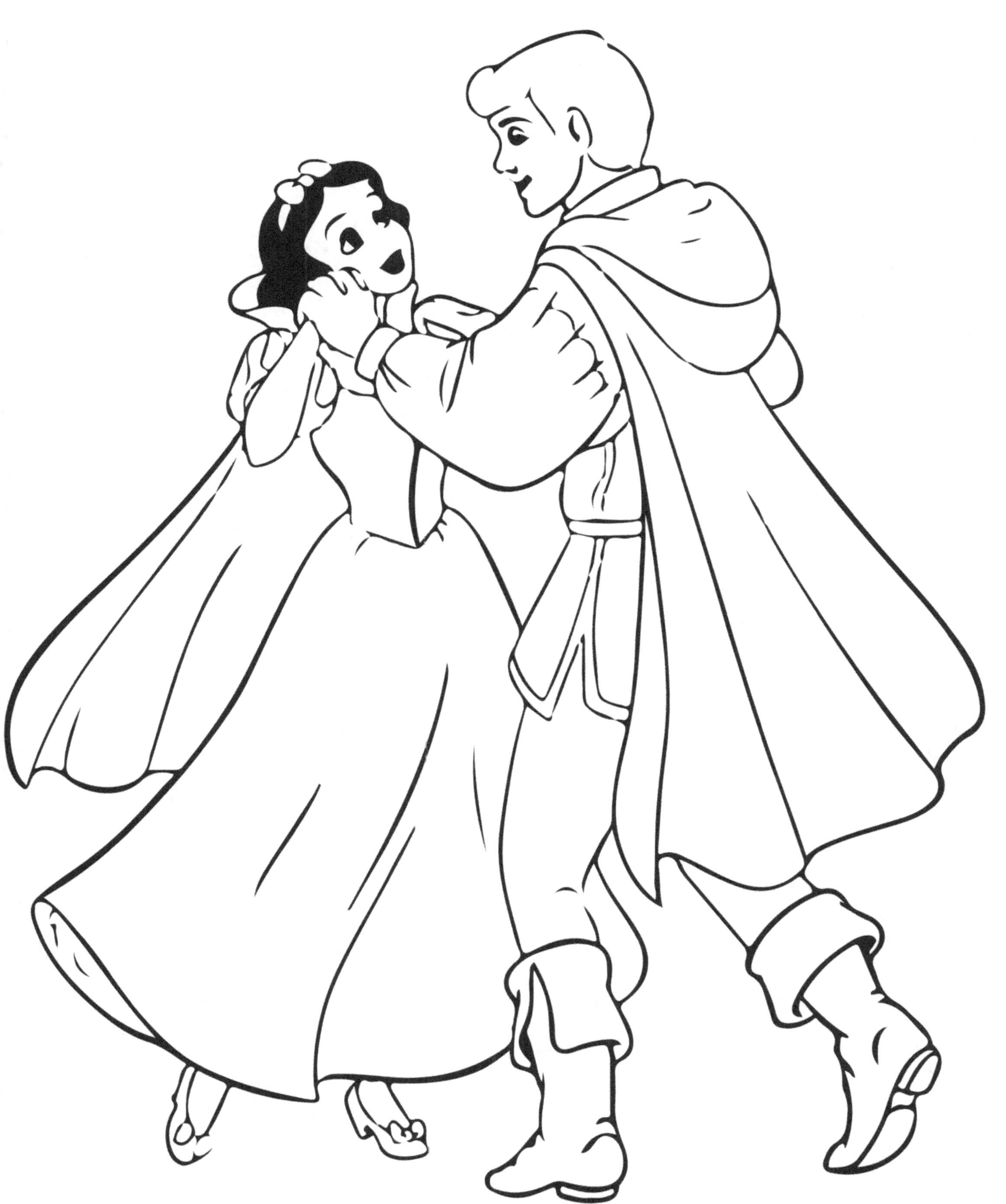

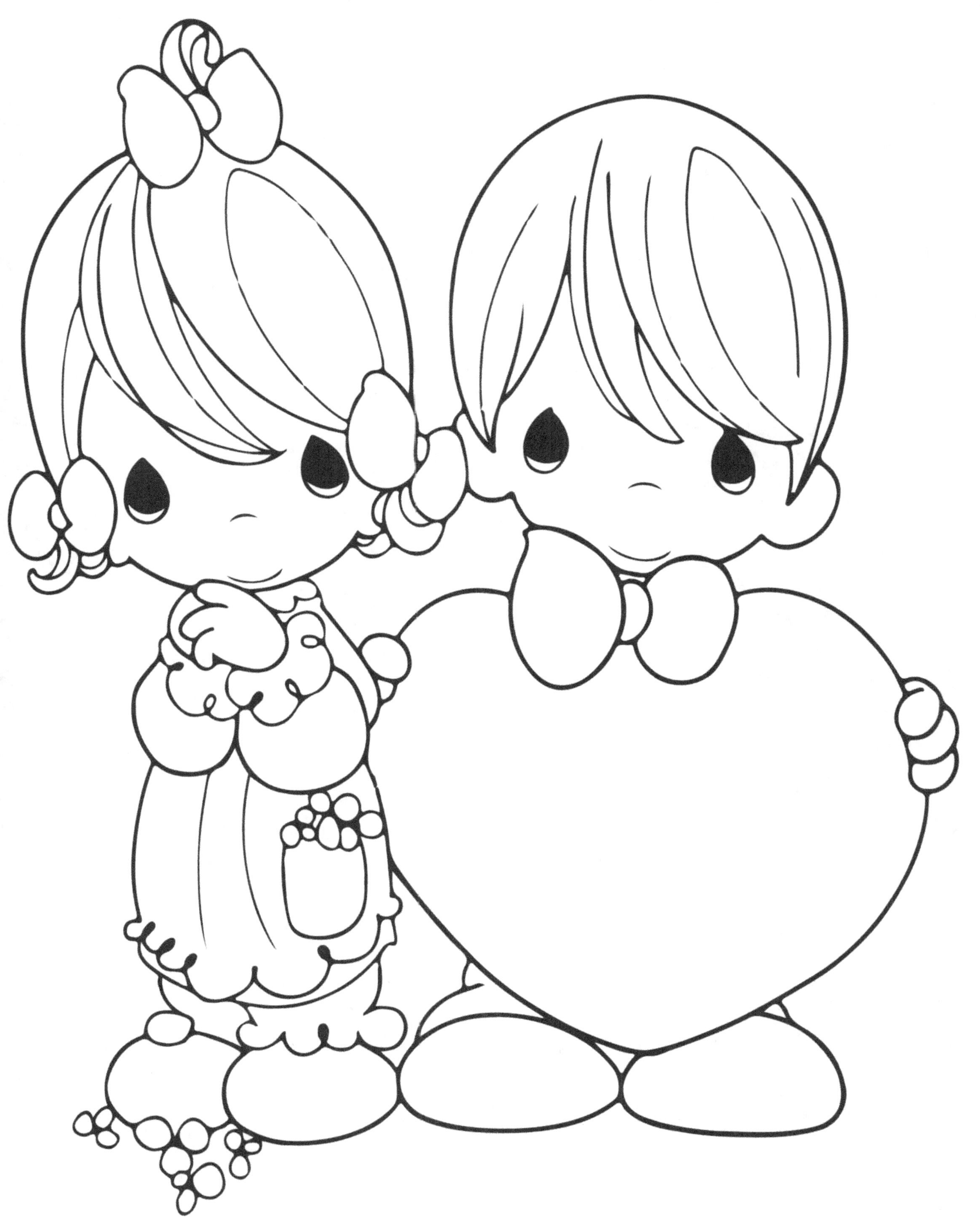

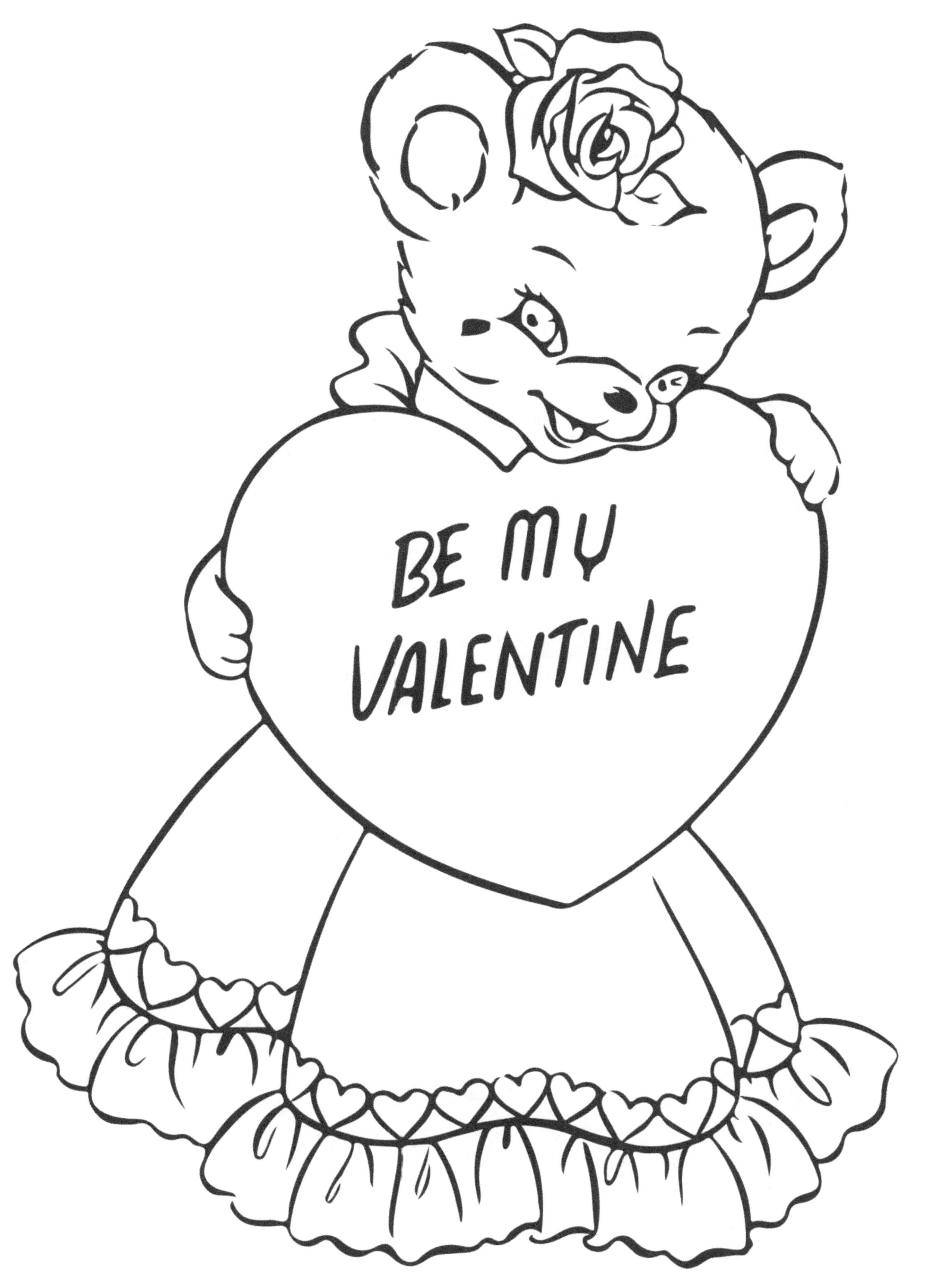

BE MY
VALENTINE

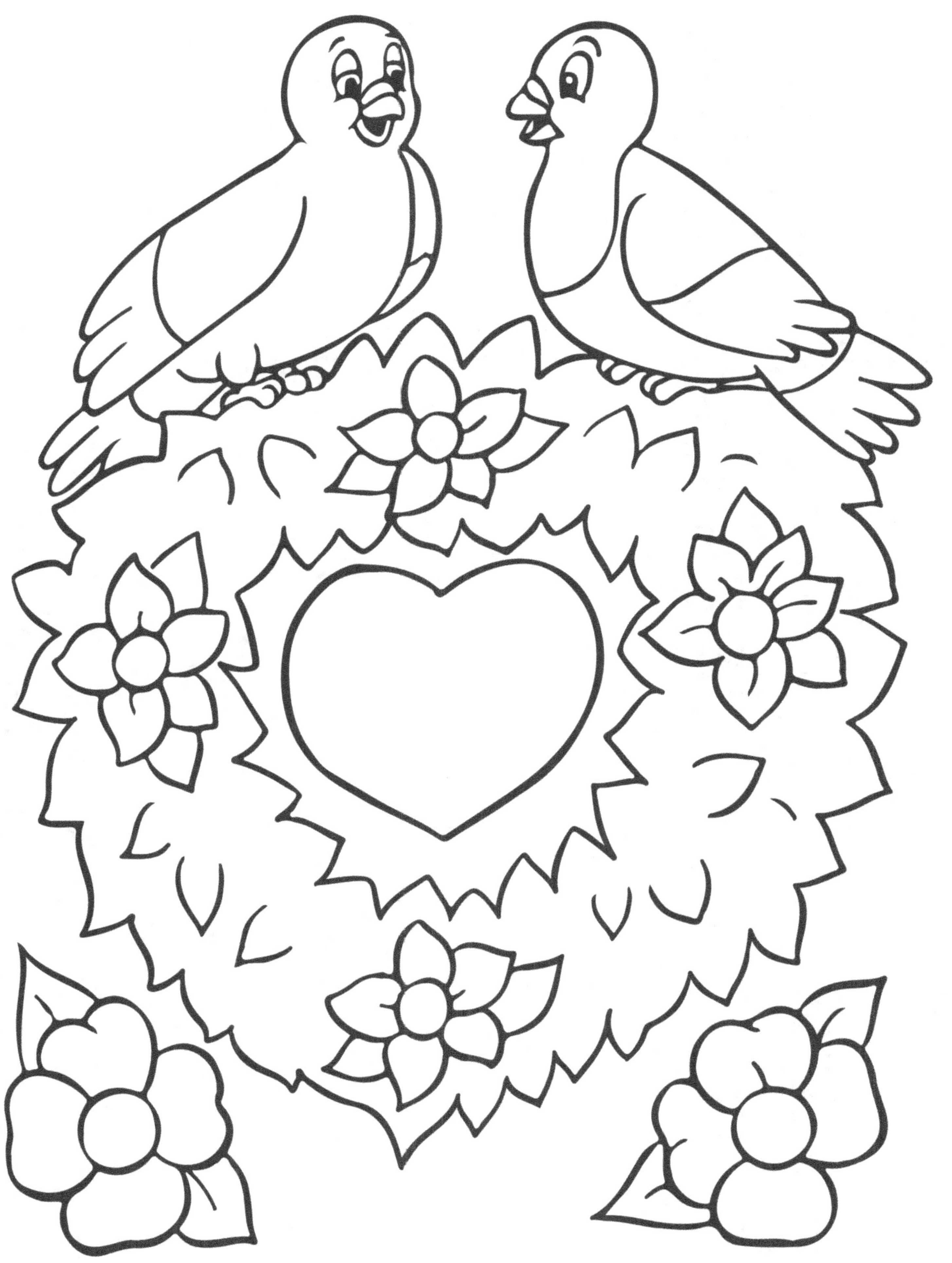

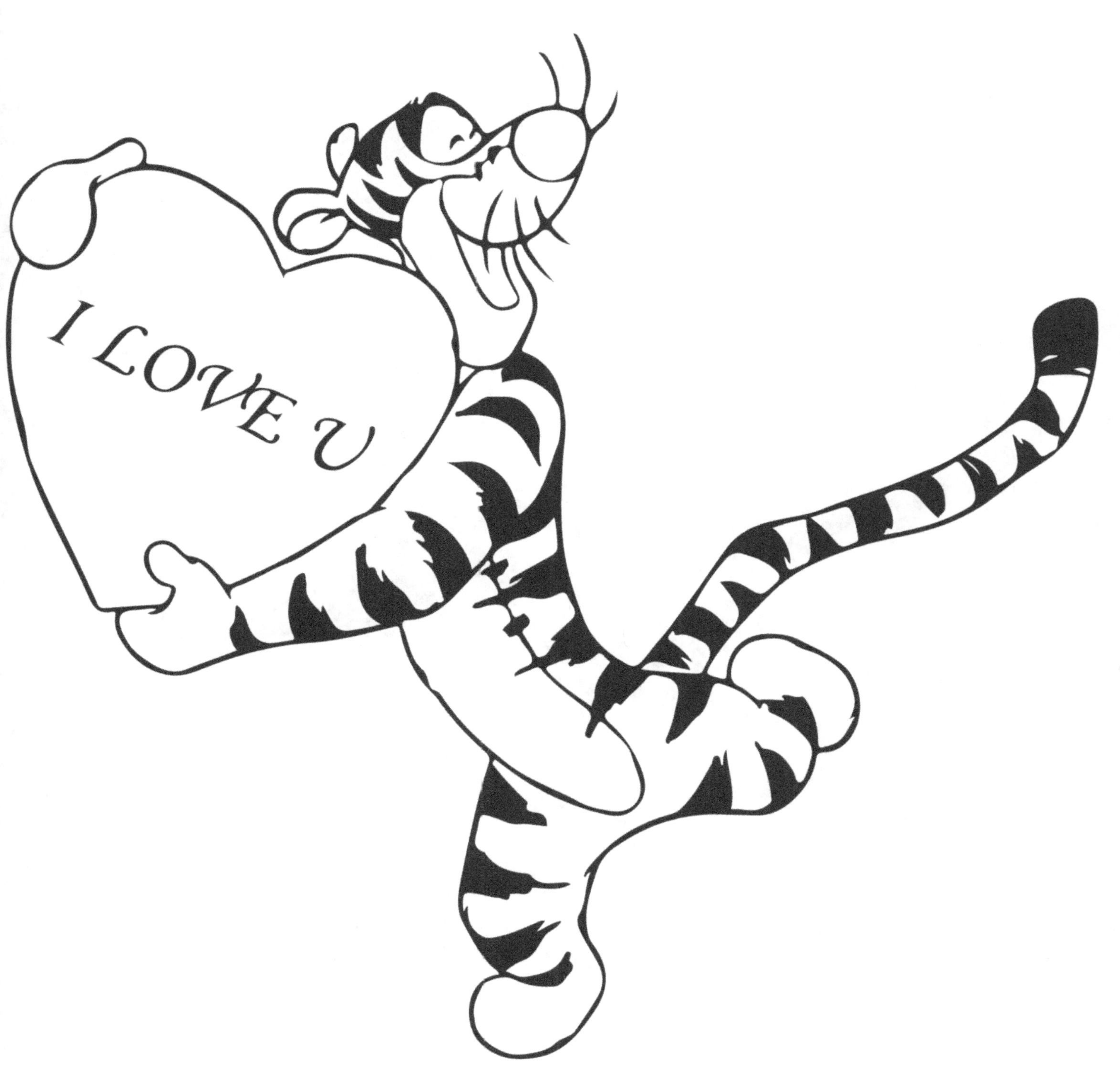

I LOVE U

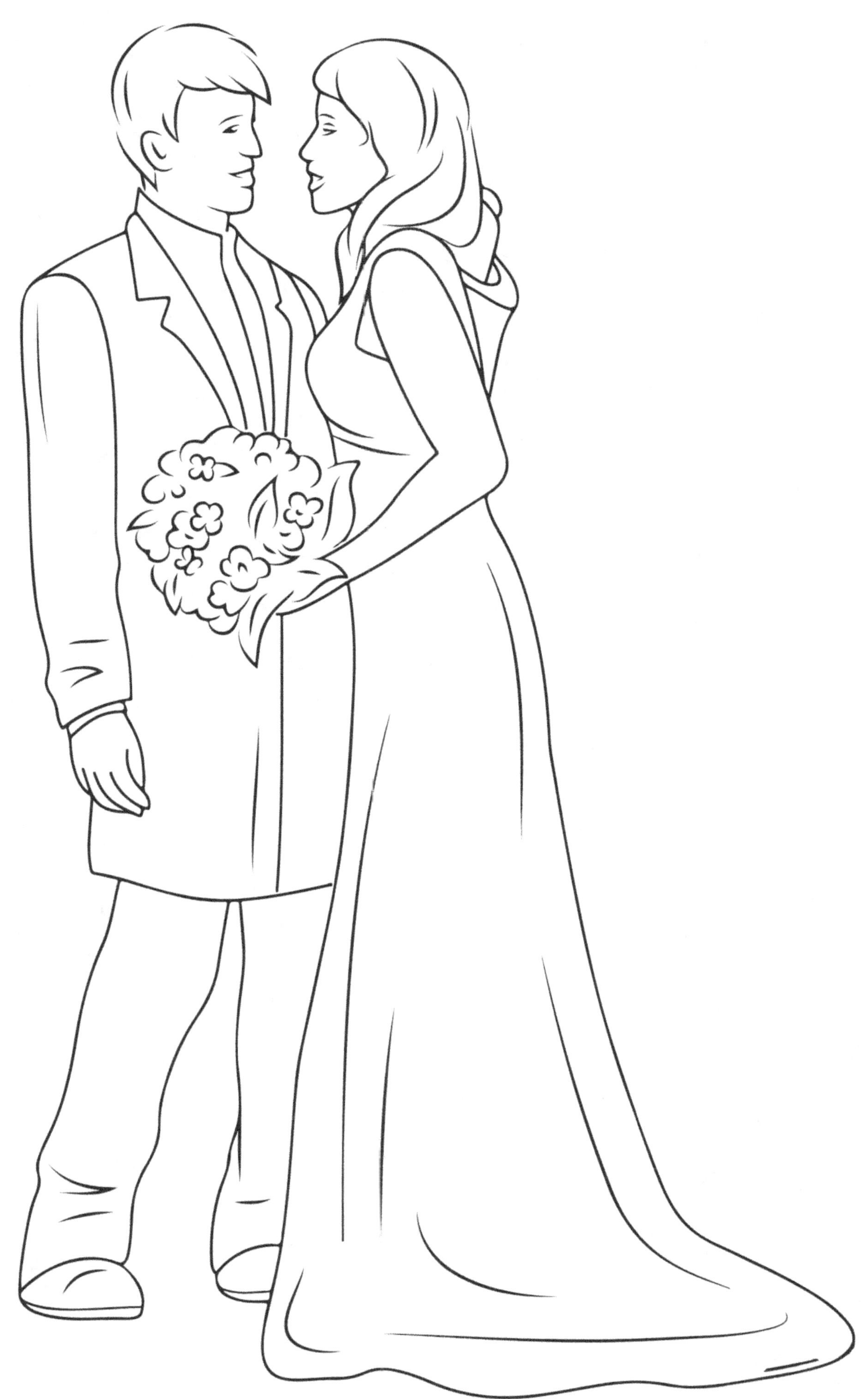

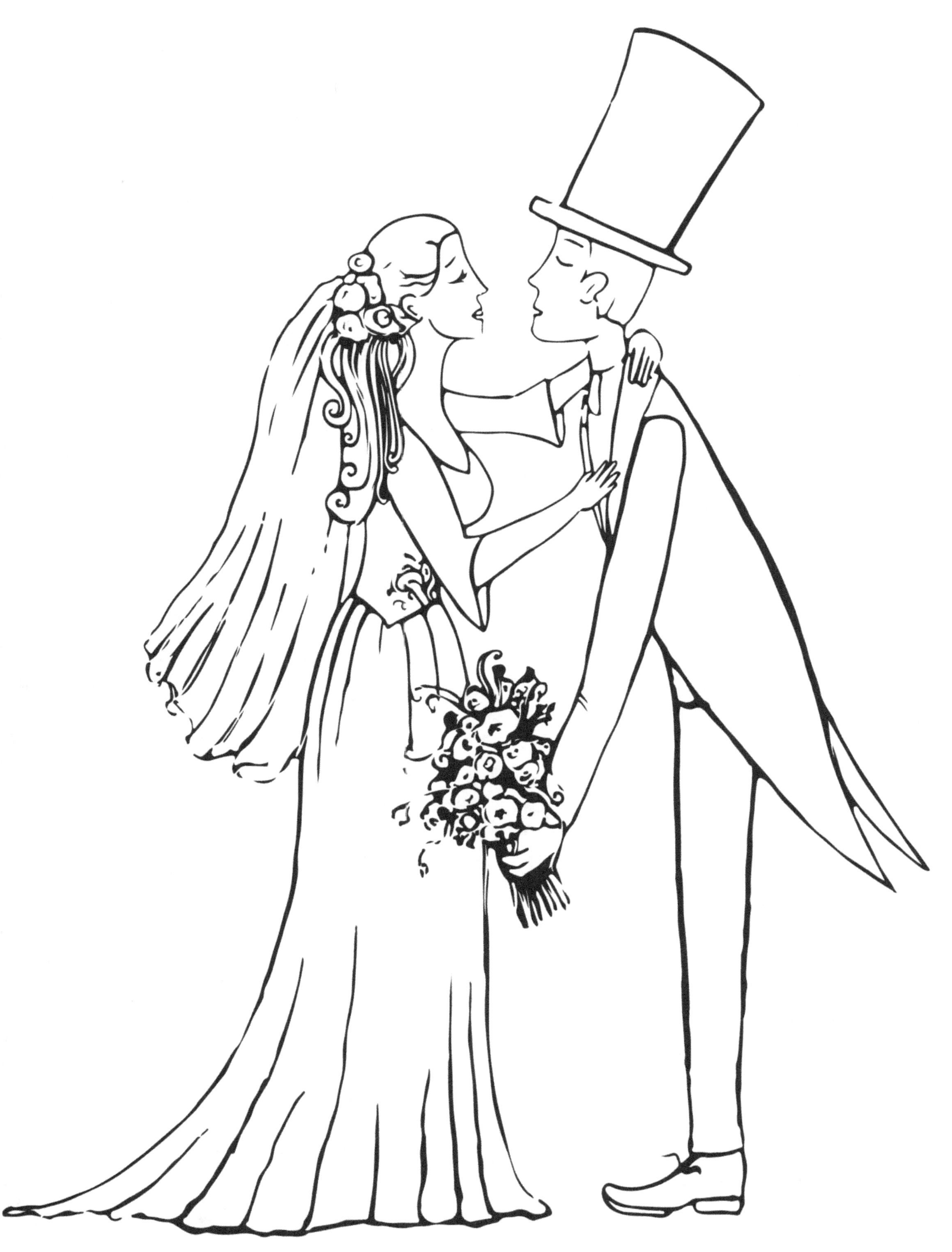

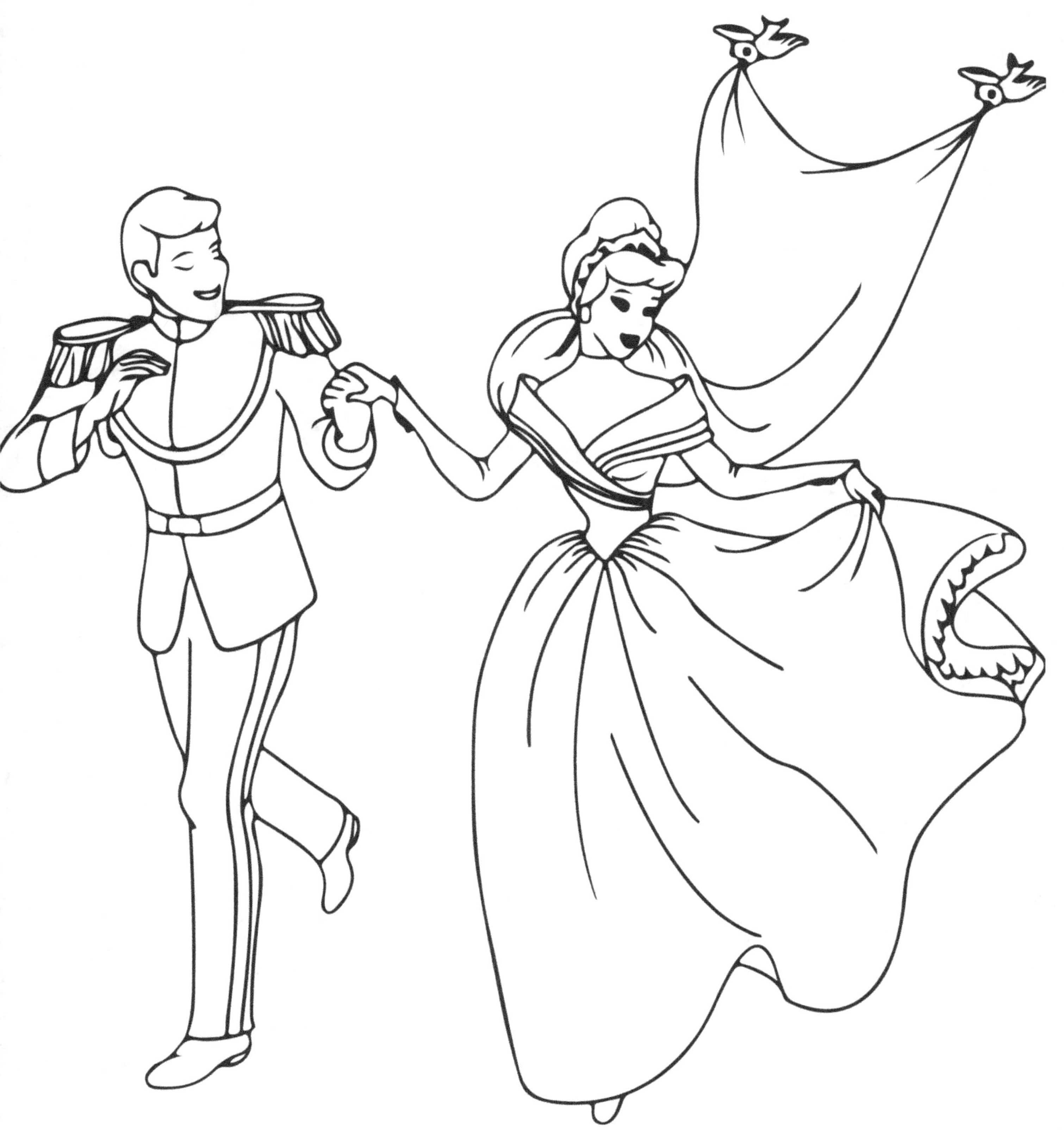

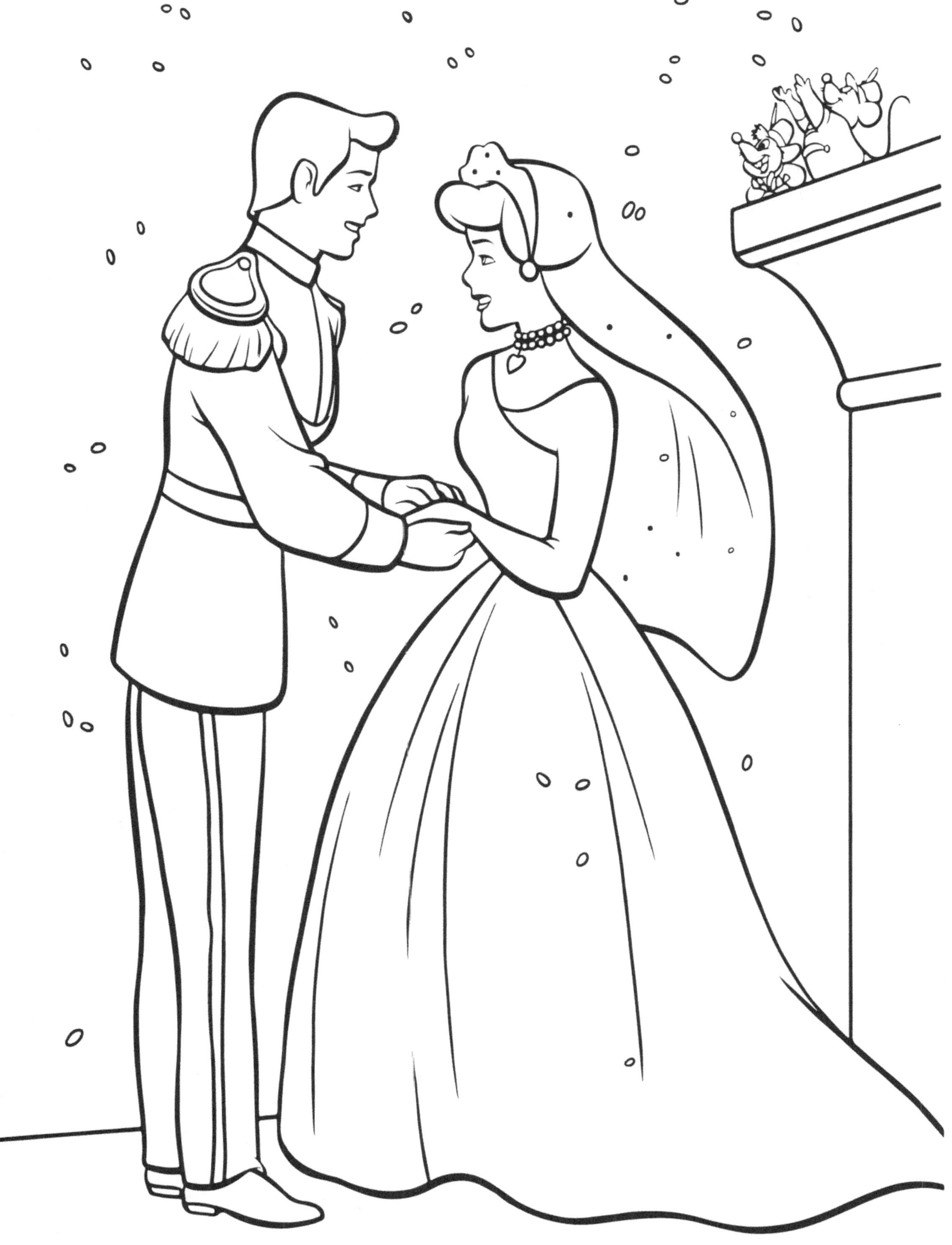

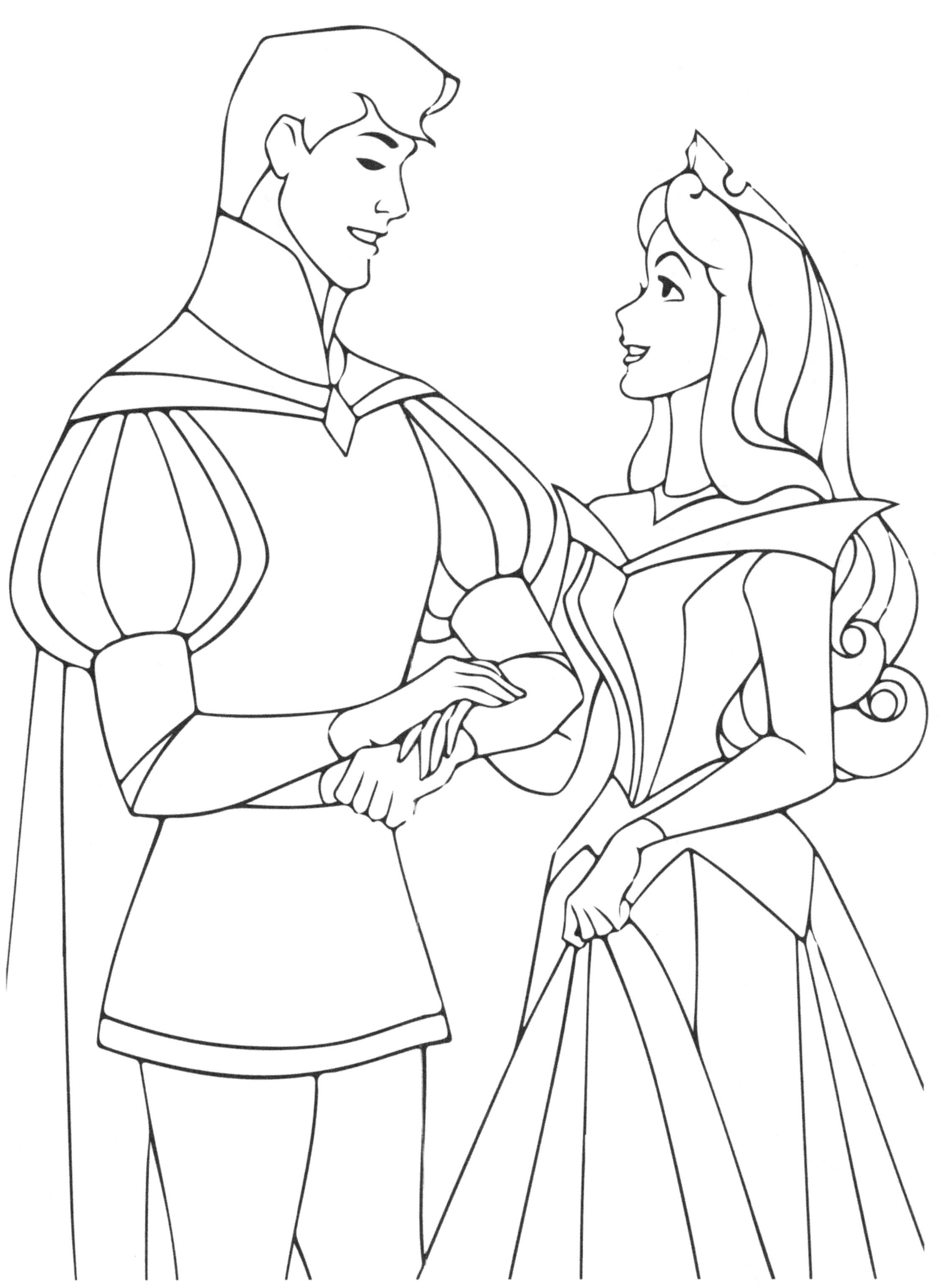

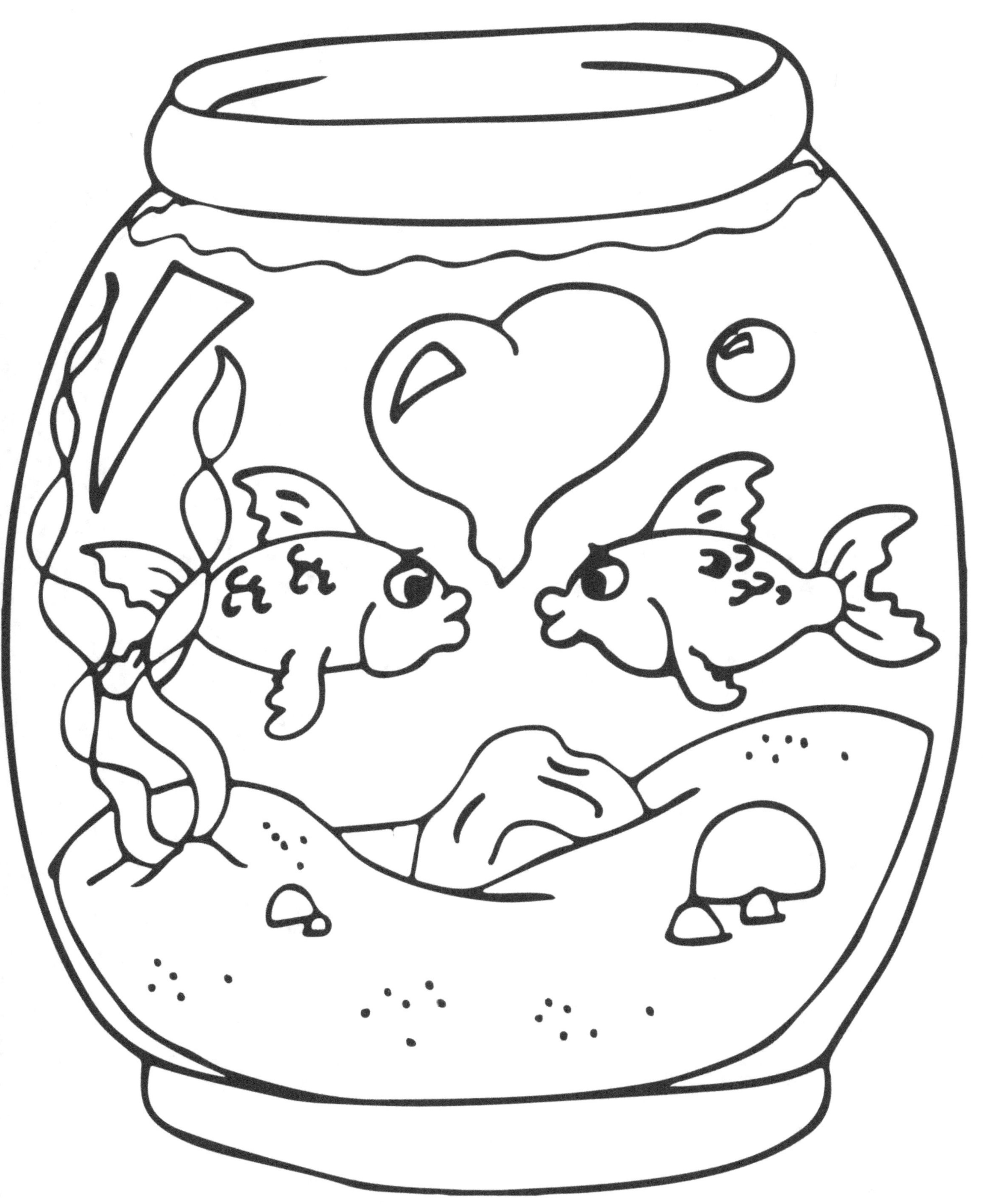

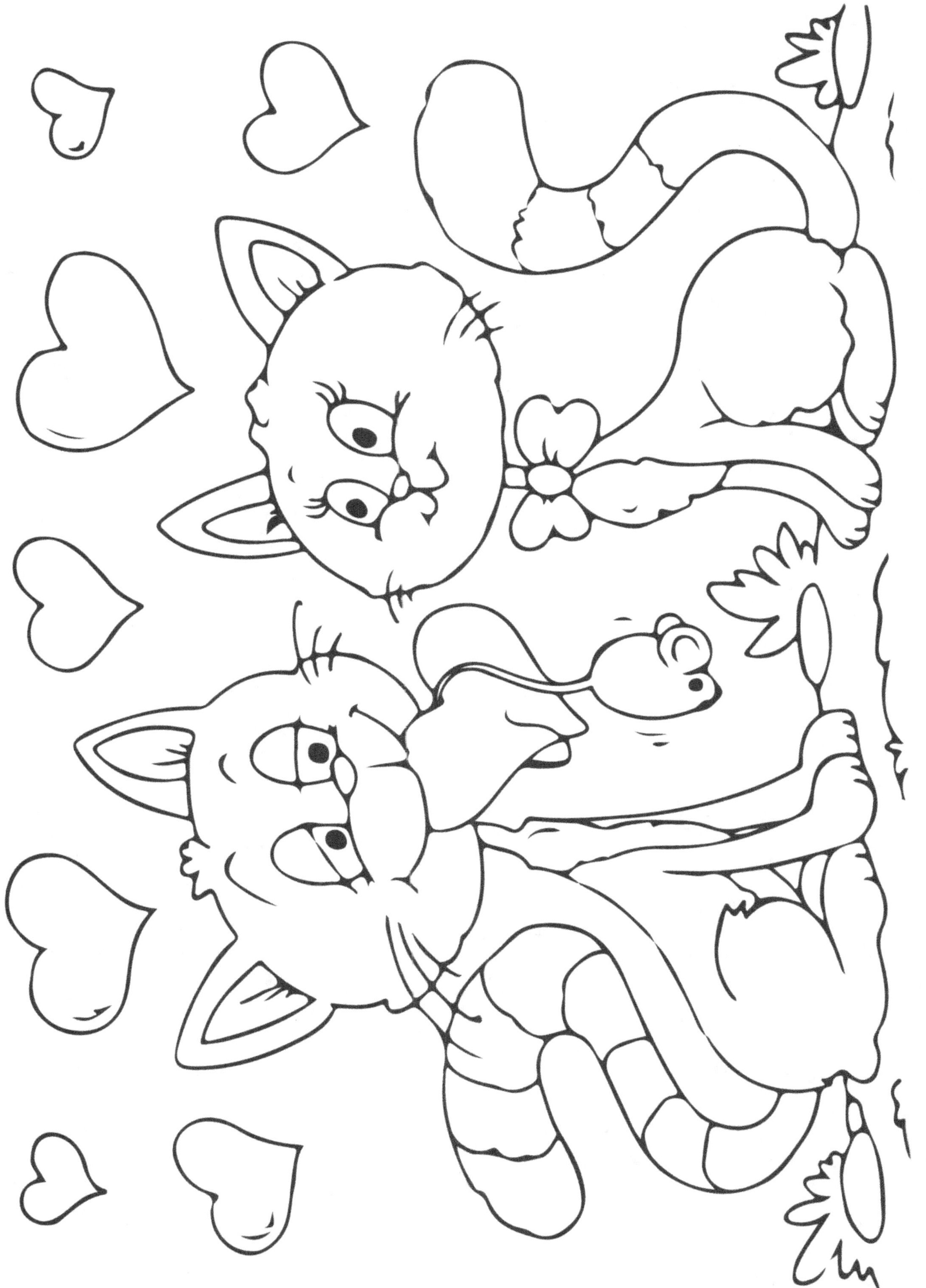

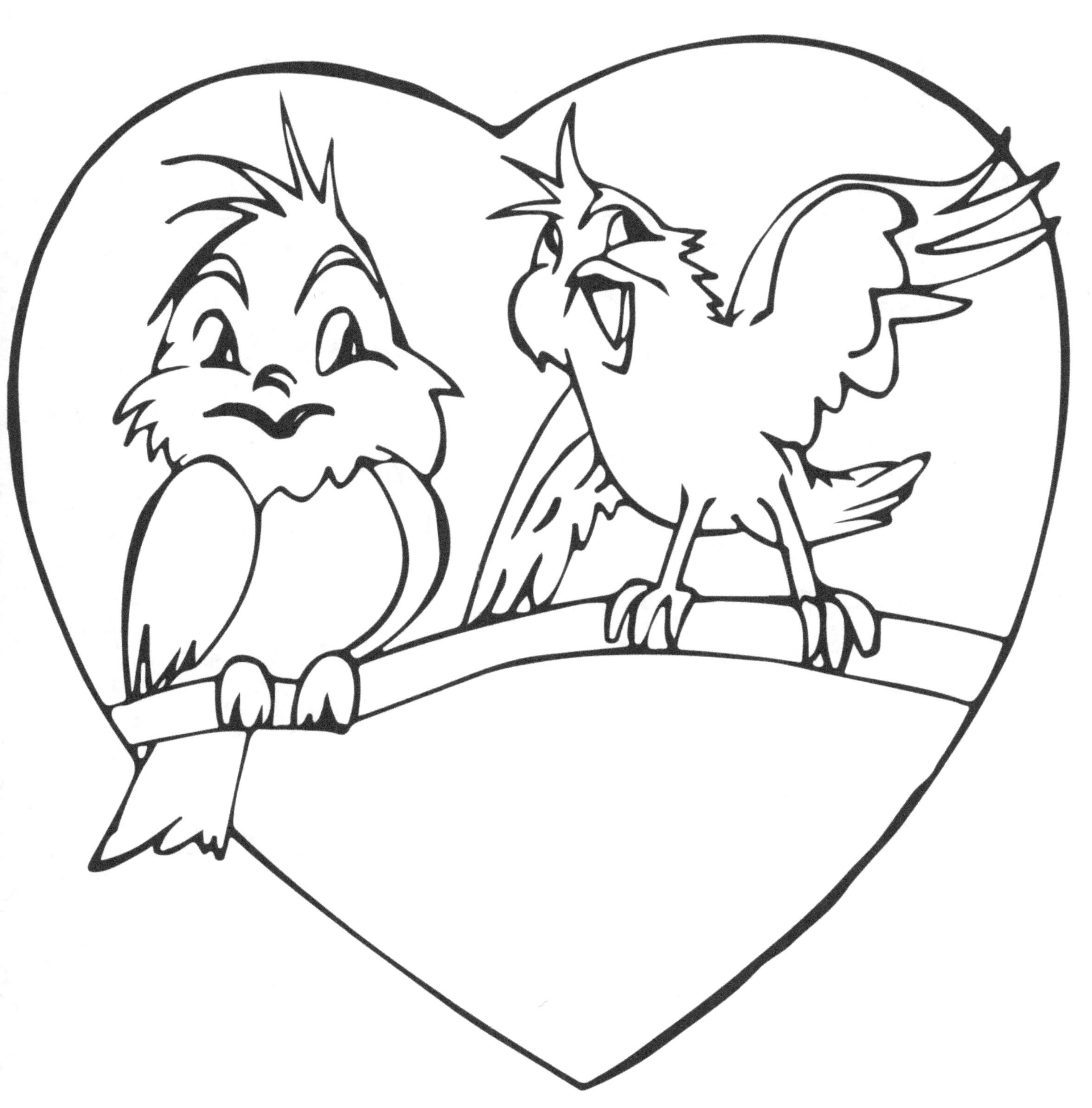

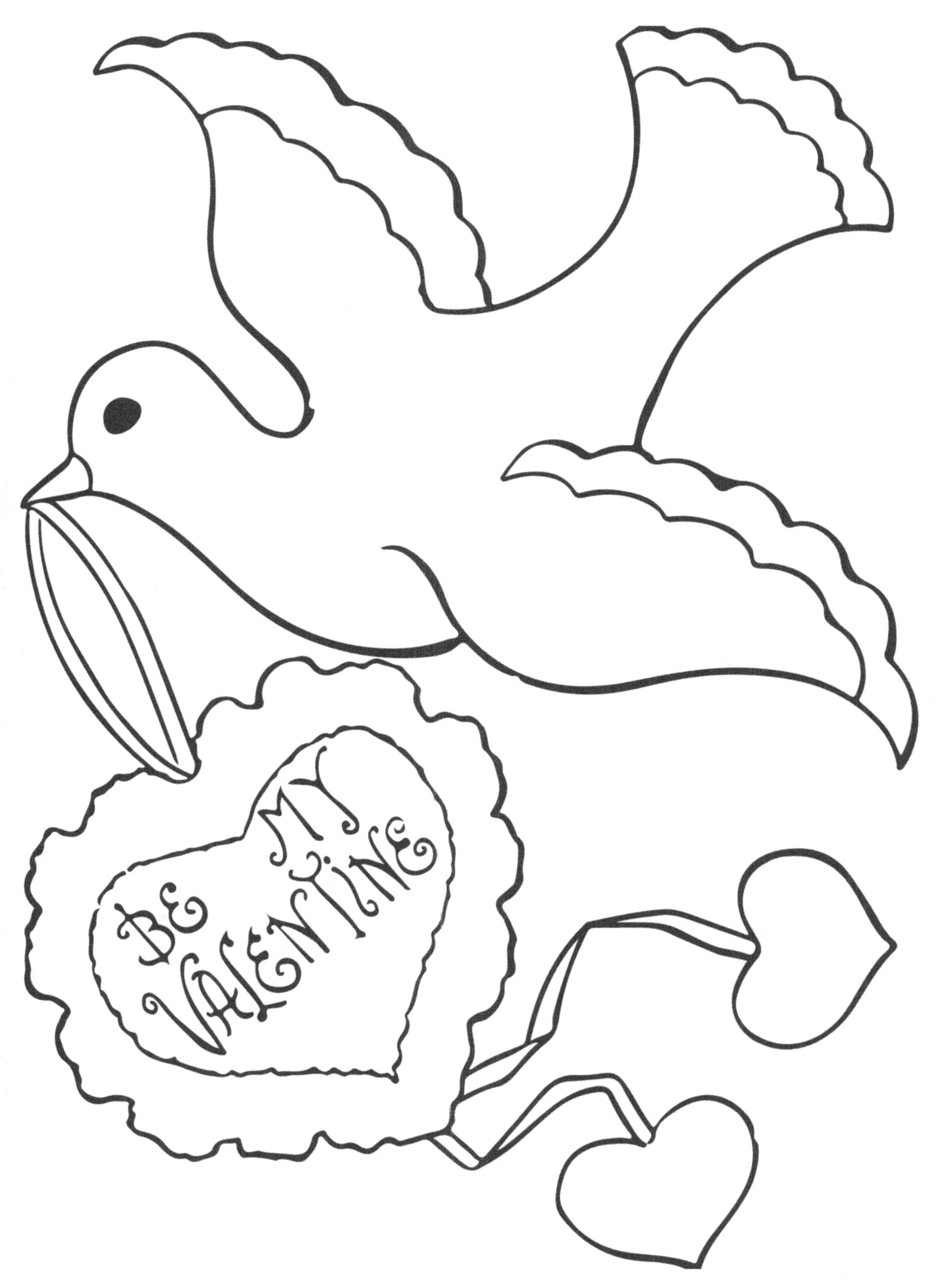

BE MY
VALENTINE

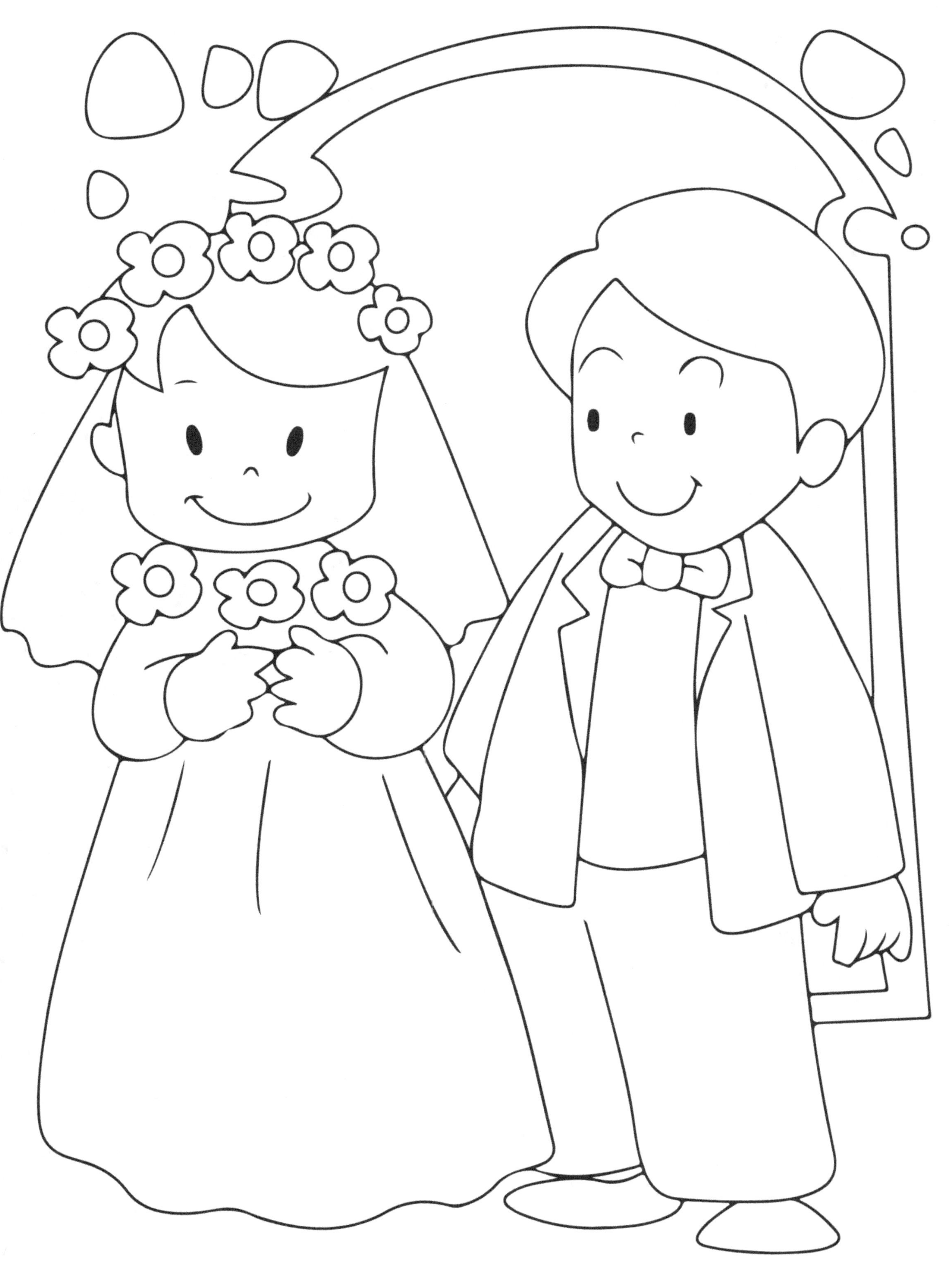

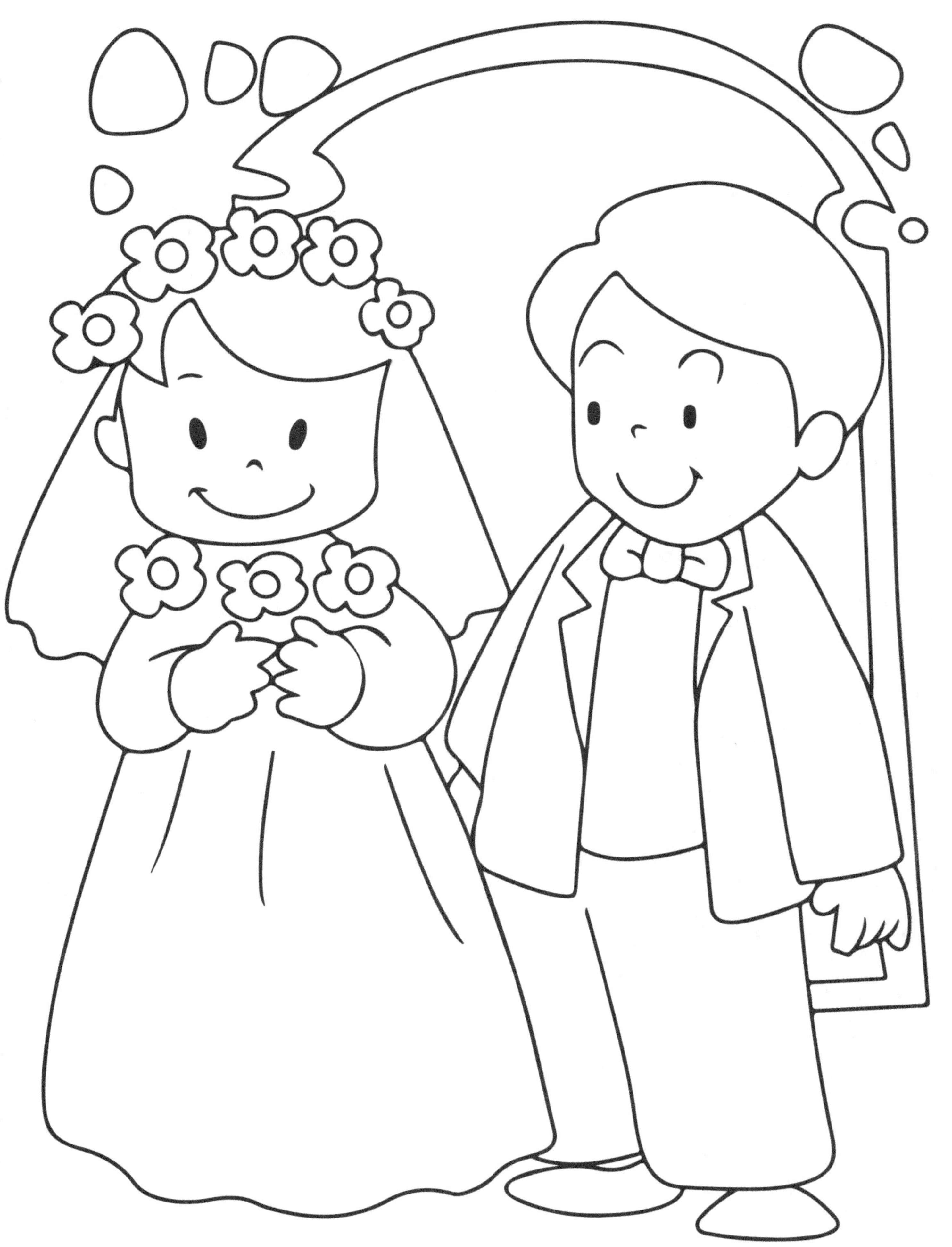

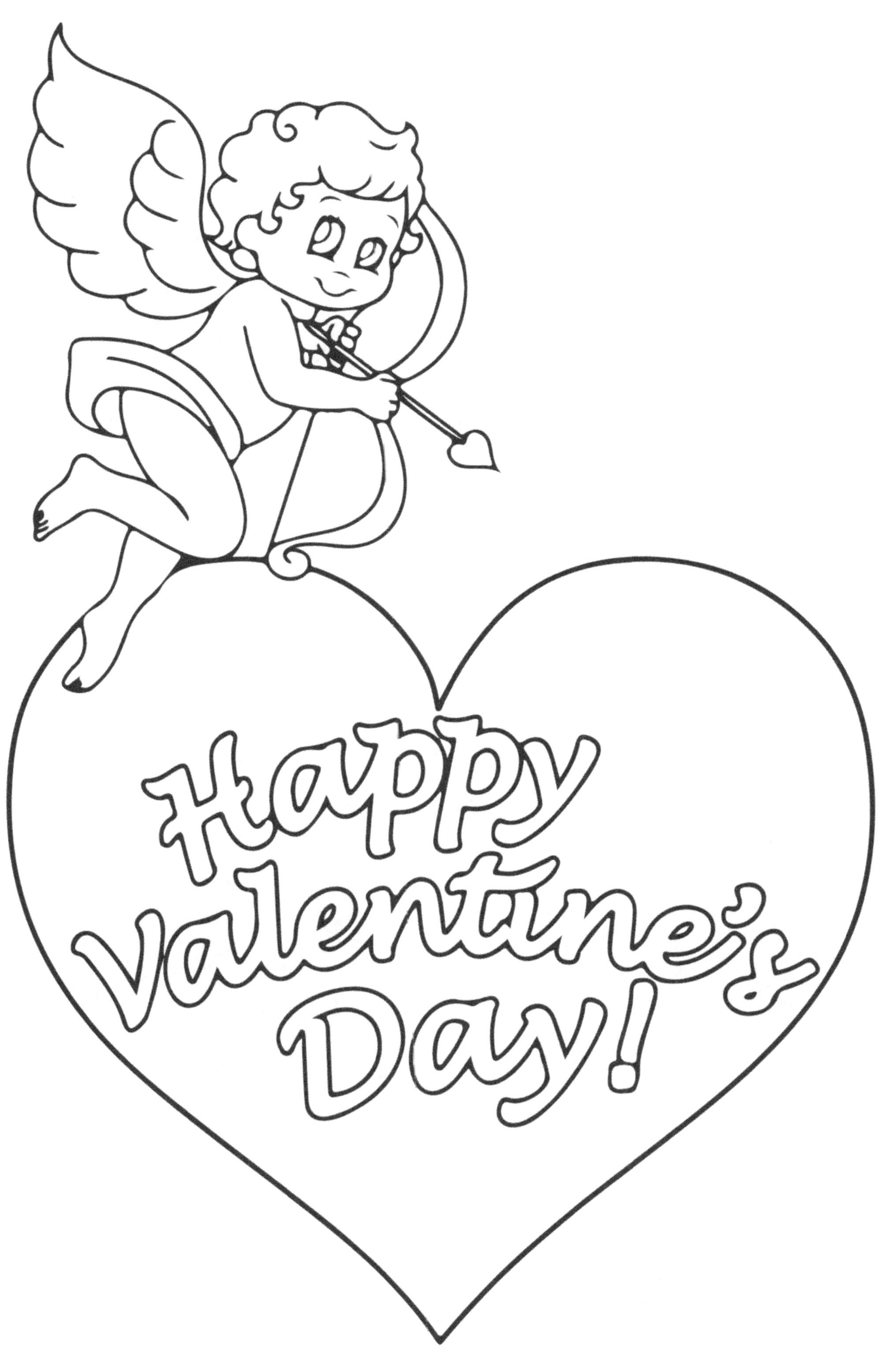

Happy Valentine's Day!

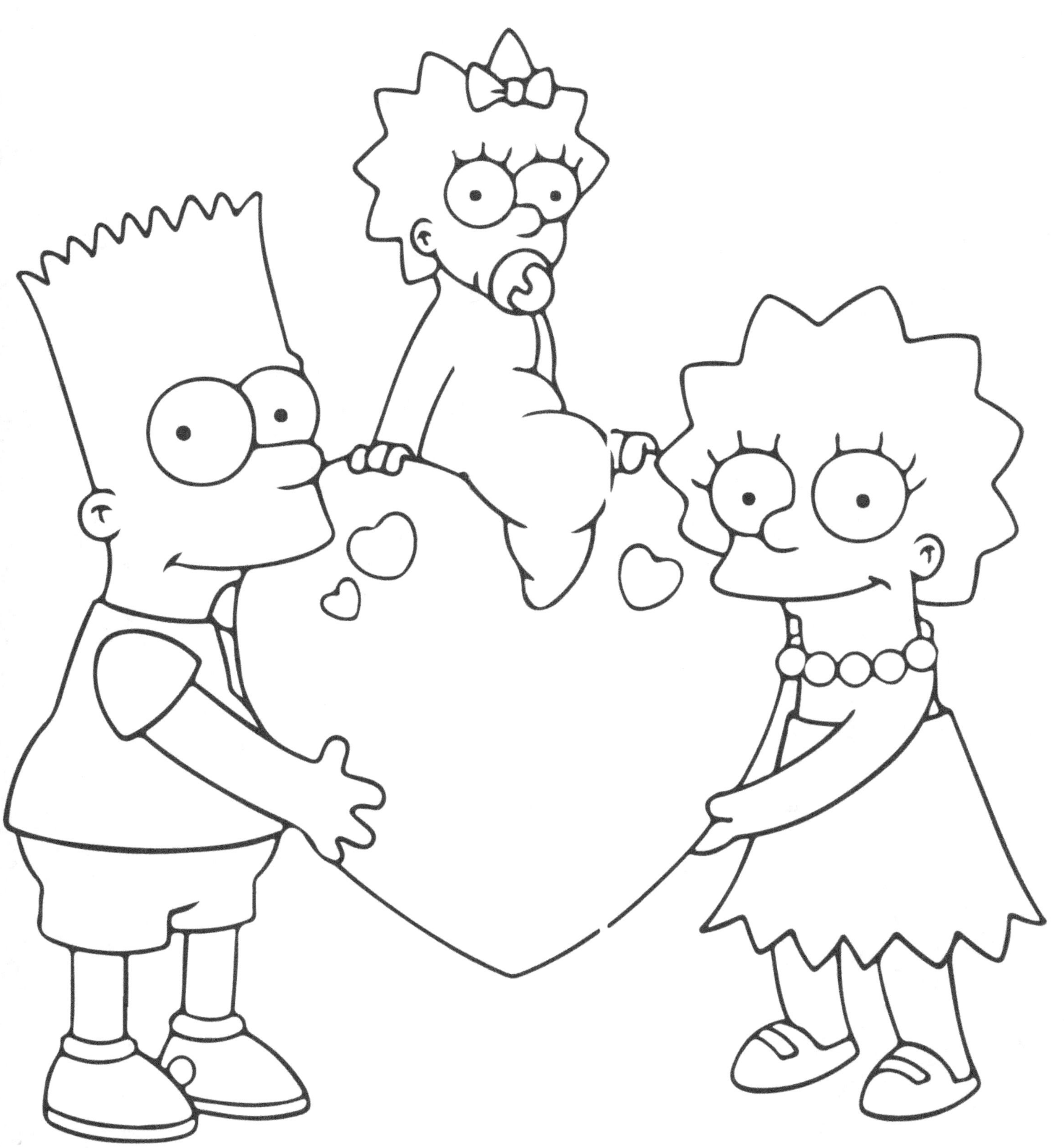

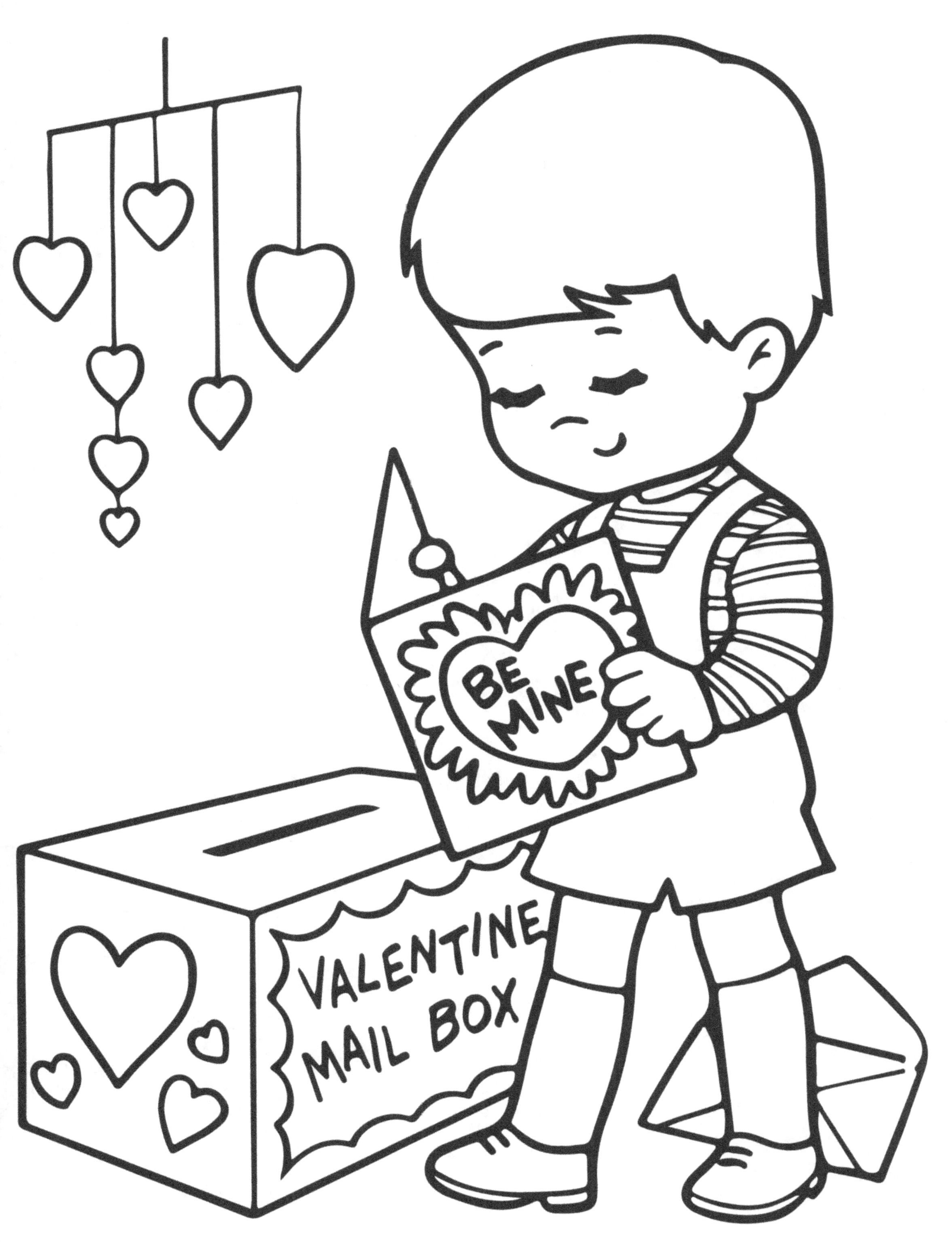

BE MINE
VALENTINE
MAIL BOX

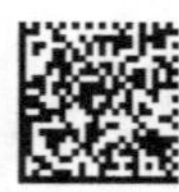